AF610830

Probate
A Personal Journey

Philip Wadner

2015

Published by Cade Books

ISBN 978-0-9931987-1-7

www.cadebooks.co.uk

This book is dedicated to Hilda Brooker
(1920 - 2012)

Disclaimer: Please note that I am not a legal practitioner and information in this guide is based upon my personal experience and understanding of how to obtain grant of probate. It is intended only to show that it is possible for someone outside the legal profession to obtain probate with neither much stress nor great expense. If you doubt your capabilities, or you need to deal with a house sale or investments, or the directions in the will are complicated or ambiguous, then please seek professional advice. I accept no responsibility should your attempt end in tears!

Contents

Probate
A Personal Journey

Introduction

Sad to say that we lost mother-in-law in early summer. She had seen just short of ninety two years pass by, although didn't relate to the last few because of Alzheimer's disease. To watch someone who was great with figures, with a keen wit, who loved her crosswords, and cherished books, have all of that stolen by this cruel disease was heart breaking.

After looking after her financial affairs for many years under a power of attorney, the family agreed that we should have sufficient knowledge to obtain probate on her estate.

When I say 'we' here, I was well aware that the bulk of the work would fall to me. Which was finc. I'm quite good at form filling, shuffling paperwork, keeping records and planning! I was joint executor with my sister-in-law, and as it happens I had prepared the wills for both my father-in-law and mother-in-law many years earlier so was very familiar with the content.

Another very good reason for me to take the driving seat was that this was a difficult time emotionally for the family. I felt a great affection for mother-in-law but, unlike her daughters who were deeply affected by her passing, for me there was an element of detachment.

All in all, it seemed a natural choice to use the DIY route to obtain grant of probate, and for me to get on and do it.

Grant of probate, or letters of administration? The answer to this question was clear cut. There was a valid will, and there were two executors named in it. In order to obtain the authority needed to share out the estate, a grant of probate was needed. Had there not been a valid will, or there were no executors named, or the executors did not wish to act, then letters of administration would have been required to distribute the estate.

Is it really necessary to obtain grant of probate? This may seem a pointless question, but why bother if it's not required? The answer was not as straightforward as I thought it might be. For instance, on the death of a partner, it is quite possible that probate would not be required. If all the money is held in joint bank accounts, or the value of money in a sole account is very small, probate is unlikely to be needed. Often, the largest element of an estate will be property, but if it is owned as joint tenants then the surviving partner will automatically inherit it. However, if the property is owned as tenants in common, different rules apply. If you think that probate may not be required, it is worth a quick phone call to the institutions concerned just to make sure. For example, ask the bank if it is willing to release the funds of the deceased without seeing a grant of probate?

For a fleeting moment, we wondered whether having had power of attorney would make things easier to sort out. However, don't be tempted by this thought because any power of attorney becomes null and void once the donor has died. The fact that we had been looking after mother-in-law's finances for many years made it more important that we applied for grant of probate, not less, as that would ensure that everything was out in the open and a matter of record.

So I started out on what I thought could be a long and difficult journey. At least, that's what the legal profession might have us believe. My target to complete the work was three months, which was fairly arbitrary. I believe it's always a good idea to set a goal as it helps with momentum and also brings an urgency to any discussions with other parties, even if the target is to a large extent artificial.

I kept a weekly diary of what happened, and have published it here not as a typical 'How To' guide, but as a record of my personal journey. I hope it might encourage others to take the plunge. There was no point in writing down detailed instructions about how to fill in the various forms, because this would be slightly different for everyone. There is plenty of guidance readily available on relevant web sites, and many books written on the subject. I have, however, noted any snags I found on the way and have included a few retrospective notes.

It probably isn't necessary to mention it, but anyone setting out on this journey should be aware that it is one that holds huge responsibility. By naming you as executor, the deceased person has placed all of their trust in you to carry out the wishes contained in their will to your very best ability. It is not a responsibility that should be taken lightly.

This is a record of how it went for me.

Week 1

I appreciated that there were quite a few gaps in my knowledge of 'probate', so a couple of books seemed to be in order.

One was already on the bookshelf – *Wills and Probate*, published by Which?, ISBN 9780340486047. As with most Which? publications, the book is a comfortable read. Checking the date inside, I found it to be a 1988 edition, near enough a quarter of century old. The first section covered will writing, and it rapidly dawned on me that I must have used this same book to help with preparing the DIY wills!

Reckoning I needed to be brought up to date, I purchased *Probate – The Guide to Obtaining Grant of Probate and Administering an Estate*, written by Gordon Bowley and published by How To Books Ltd. ISBN is 9781845284091. To be honest, I found this book contained little that wasn't either straightforward common sense or that I didn't already know from general knowledge picked up over the years. It did, however, have a handy appendix with some specimen letters, of which there were sure to be many, and reading through most of the chapters gave me a warm feeling that all would go well.

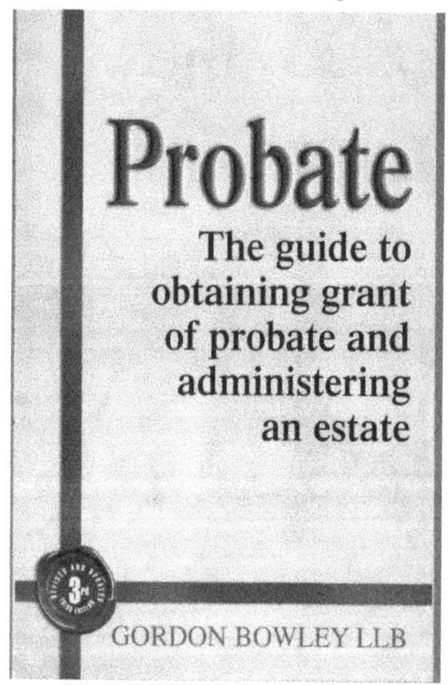

My first job was to produce a rough idea of what would be involved, so the beginning of what would probably be an endless 'to do' list was created:

For example, I would need to sift through all the old papers looking for insurance policies, bank books, premium bonds and the like. It would also be necessary to take a guess at the value of personal belongings (there was no house and little furniture to consider). On the other side of the coin, I would have to note any outstanding bills and accounts, and estimate the final cost of the funeral, probate fees and other expenses likely to be incurred. All of this would be required to produce a rough estimate of the size of the estate

Because we had power of attorney in recent years, most of this information was easy to gather together with considerable accuracy. In fact, as the house had already been sold and its contents cleared, we had everything needed stored safely away. It was just a matter of looking in the right boxes!

*Update: When we sold the house, we arranged for the post to be diverted. If you need to do that during the probate process, then it would seem to be a good idea to arrange it sooner rather than later. The cost can be reclaimed from the estate.

A straightforward spreadsheet (see below, but without the actual figures) provided a simple way of producing an estimated net value for the estate. Given that some amounts might increase and others could decrease, I hoped this would provide a realistic indication of the actual final value.

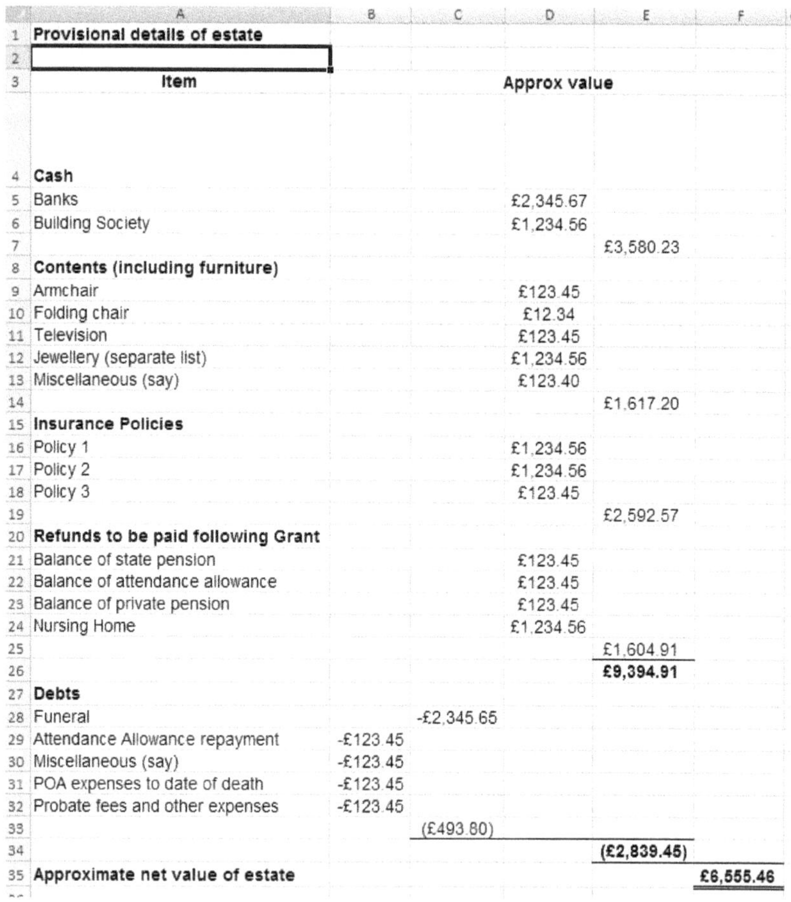

	A	B	C	D	E	F
1	**Provisional details of estate**					
2						
3	**Item**			**Approx value**		
4	**Cash**					
5	Banks			£2,345.67		
6	Building Society			£1,234.56		
7					£3,580.23	
8	**Contents (including furniture)**					
9	Armchair			£123.45		
10	Folding chair			£12.34		
11	Television			£123.45		
12	Jewellery (separate list)			£1,234.56		
13	Miscellaneous (say)			£123.40		
14					£1,617.20	
15	**Insurance Policies**					
16	Policy 1			£1,234.56		
17	Policy 2			£1,234.56		
18	Policy 3			£123.45		
19					£2,592.57	
20	**Refunds to be paid following Grant**					
21	Balance of state pension			£123.45		
22	Balance of attendance allowance			£123.45		
23	Balance of private pension			£123.45		
24	Nursing Home			£1,234.56		
25					£1,604.91	
26					**£9,394.91**	
27	**Debts**					
28	Funeral		-£2,345.65			
29	Attendance Allowance repayment	-£123.45				
30	Miscellaneous (say)	-£123.45				
31	POA expenses to date of death	-£123.45				
32	Probate fees and other expenses	-£123.45				
33			(£493.80)			
34					**(£2,839.45)**	
35	**Approximate net value of estate**					**£6,555.46**

You might think I jumped the gun a bit here, trying to produce an estate estimate so early. Well, the reason was that I called the local Probate Registry in Leicester and asked about the possibility of getting the interview for the grant in Bedford, which would be very handy for me. You can find your nearest Probate Registry by looking on this website:

https://courttribunalfinder.service.gov.uk/search/

It transpired that interviews were only held in Bedford for one day every three months, and the next one planned was just a few weeks away. It came as a surprise that they were so infrequent. The person I spoke to was very helpful and said that if I got the probate forms and inheritance tax forms in the post quickly, there was a good chance of getting an appointment for the next session.

The probate application form, and some very useful explanatory leaflets, are all available from the government website here:

http://hmctsformfinder.justice.gov.uk/HMCTS/GetForm.do?court_forms_id=735

To be honest, although there seemed to be a huge number of different leaflets, it was worth downloading and printing all of them, and reading each one thoroughly more than once. Having a printed copy meant that it was easy to make notes against the important parts not to be forgotten. Much of the information was either irrelevant or patently obvious, but just knowing I was best prepared did a lot for my confidence.

Even though the net value of the estate was small, and I was sure there would be no inheritance tax to pay, it was a surprise to find that there would still be an inheritance tax form to fill in. Just in case I was missing something, I double checked the inheritance tax thresholds on the government's website:

https://www.gov.uk/inheritance-tax

As expected, the value of the estate was well below the limit for paying inheritance tax, but I needed to fill out form IHT205 to show that this was the case and that the estate was 'excepted'. The forms (and I see that they have been updated since I used them) are available here:

https://www.gov.uk/government/publications/inheritance-tax-return-of-estate-information-iht205-2011

Pulling up the estate value spreadsheet prepared earlier, I arranged a simple cross reference against the categories needed on the IHT form. Not only did that help with understanding how the government regards the various categories of estate value, but it would also make it easy to look back at the basis of the figures should there be any future queries.

	A	B	C	D	E	F	H	I	J	K	L	M	N	O	P	Q	R	S
1	**Provisional details of estate**																	
2																		
3	**Item**			**Approx value**			**Transferred to IHT205(2006)**											
							11.1 Cash	**11.2 Personal goods**	**11.5 Insurance Policies**	**11.6 Money owed to deceased**	**Box D Gross Value**	**12.1 Funeral**	**12.3 Debts**	**Box E Debts**	**Box F Net Estate Value**	**Box G Net Estate for IHT**	**Box H Gross Value for IHT**	**Box K Net Qualifying Value**
4	**Cash**																	
5	Banks			£2,345.67			**£3,580.23**	**£1,617.20**	**£2,592.57**	**£1,604.91**	**£9,394.91**	**(£2,345.65)**	**(£493.80)**	**(£2,839.45)**	**£6,555.46**	**£6,555.46**	**£9,394.91**	**£6,555.46**
6	Building Society			£1,234.56														
7					£3,580.23		£3,580.23											
8	**Contents (including furniture)**																	
9	Armchair			£123.45														
10	Folding chair			£12.34														
11	Television			£123.45														
12	Jewellery (separate list)			£1,234.56														
13	Miscellaneous (say)			£123.40														
14					£1,617.20			£1,617.20										
15	**Insurance Policies**																	
16	Policy 1			£1,234.56														
17	Policy 2			£1,234.56														
18	Policy 3			£123.45														
19					£2,592.57				£2,592.57									
20	**Refunds to be paid following Grant**																	
21	Balance of state pension			£123.45														
22	Balance of attendance allowance			£123.45														
23	Balance of private pension			£123.45														
24	Nursing Home			£1,234.56														
25					£1,604.91					£1,604.91								
26					**£9,394.91**						£9,394.91							
27	**Debts**																	
28	Funeral		-£2,345.65									(£2,345.65)						
29	Attendance Allowance repayment	-£123.45																
30	Miscellaneous (say)	-£123.45																
31	POA expenses to date of death	-£123.45																
32	Probate fees and other expenses	-£123.45																
33			(£493.80)										(£493.80)					
34					**(£2,839.45)**									(£2,839.45)				
35	**Approximate net value of estate**					**£6,555.46**									£6,555.46	£6,555.46	£9,394.91	£6,555.46

This was already turning out to be quite a busy first week, and I began to wonder whether my three month target had been a bit optimistic. The next important item to deal with was the probate form PA1. Had there not been the urgency to make the next probate interview, with the next being three months away, the pace could have relaxed a little. The PA1 form asks for basic particulars, such as the names of the deceased and their relatives, the executors of the will, and details of the person applying for the grant of probate. No problems there, so I assembled the pack for the Probate Office, took it to the Post Office and sent it off by Special Delivery. This is what was included:

- PA1 Probate Application Form
- IHT205 Inheritance Tax Form
- Original Will (not a copy)
- Original Death Certificate (not a copy)
- Cheque for the full amount required

It's worth noting a potential snag with the PA1 form. There is a handy checklist on the back page, where you can tick off all the items which need to go into the envelope. Although there is a box to enter the total for the probate fees (this depends on how many 'grants' you need to claim the money owed to the estate from banks, building societies, insurance companies, etc), there is no tick box for the actual cheque. And, of course, I forgot to include it. Even worse, I didn't realise until I had returned home and found the cheque on my desk.

Although I was doubtful they would be able to help, I searched everywhere for the phone number of the local post office. There was no record anywhere of a local phone number, only a central service. However, the person I spoke to agreed to call our local office and try to speak to the person who had served me. Fortunately I could give her name as I am a regular customer, and I also knew she would remember the transaction. After five very long minutes, the phone rang and I was told that the envelope hadn't yet passed into the postal system. So it was a case of hurrying back, retrieving the envelopc, opening it carefully and slipping the cheque inside!

Incidentally, the sealed copies were so inexpensive it's worth making sure you order enough to cover all of the organisations who may need one to release any funds due to the estate, and maybe a couple extra. Finding later that you're short of one will mean a long wait and greater expense. I ordered ten, plus two spares. That covered the insurance companies, banks, pension companies and government departments such as the Department for Work and Pensions. In the event, I had four left over but it seemed better to have more than enough than run short and hold up the process.

Although it feels as though I should have done this earlier, at the end of the first week I sent off letters to the various banks, building societies, pension providers, the Department for Work and Pensions and insurance companies to inform them of our sad news and asking for advice about what they needed in order to complete formalities. I decided to send death certificates only to the insurance companies at this point, as we had only ordered five and I didn't have enough to send to everyone. Just to be on the safe side, I made some copies myself and took them to the Post Office to have them certified as copies of the original document.

*Update: I have just checked, and the Post Office will no longer certify death certificates under their checking service, so make sure you have sufficient from the registrar where the death was recorded.

In the event, by careful juggling between recipients, I only needed the five originals, and eventually had them all returned to me.

An example of one of the letters:

Stevenage
SG1

16th June, 2012

Dear Sir,

Policy numbers and , Life assured: Mrs

You will be sorry to hear that Mrs died on 10th April. I enclose a copy of the death certificate which I would be grateful if you would kindly return.

From your records you will see that I held power of attorney for Mrs . I am also one of the executors of her estate, and her daughter is the other.

Please provide details of all policies which Mrs held with you, whether solely or jointly with another person, and notify me of their value and the amount which they will yield. I need this information to prepare the estate net value prior to applying for Grant of Probate.

Please forward a claim form if you require one.

Once the Grant is obtained, I will send a copy to you so that the assets can be released.

I look forward to hearing from you.

Yours faithfully,

Philip Wadner

The Co-operative Insurance
Customer services
Miller Street
Manchester
M60 0AL

Enc: Copy of death certificate

This has seemed a frantic week, but I have only clocked up about 12 hours of actual activity. I spent about £132, most of which was to cover the probate fees and grants, and 'recorded delivery' postage. How do I know this? Because I created a simple spreadsheet for noting activities, with columns for the number of letters, emails, forms and telephone calls with additional columns to log time and expenses. This is the log so far:

	A	B	C	D	E	F	G	H
1	**Probate actions and expenses**							
2		PJW						
3		totals>	10	0	2	1	12.17	£132.45
4	Date	Activity	✉	@	▤	☎	Time	Expenses
5	11 June 2012	Produce rough plan for probate					90	
6	12 June 2012	Produce provisional net value of estate					120	
7	12 June 2012	Book - Probate: Guide to obtaining, from Amazon						£6.99
8	13 June 2012	Update provisional net value of pension portions					15	
9	13 June 2012	Call probate office Leicester for info on next interview date				1	15	£0.42
10	13 June 2012	Initial runthrough of EHT/prob forms					60	
11	14 June 2012	Letters to Nursing Care, Att All, BD8 form, postage 3x recorded dely	3				60	£4.65
12	14 June 2012	Certified copies of death certificate x3 (additional to formal copies)						£7.15
13	14 June 2012	Change estate net value items to market instead of replacement value					10	
14	14 June 2012	Pack of A5 envelopes						£3.49
15	14 June 2012	Letters to private pension schemes	2				30	
16	14 June 2012	Letters to building society and bank	2				30	
17	15 June 2012	Posted letters to private pension schemes						£3.10
18	15 June 2012	Interviews at building society andbank					45	
19	15 June 2012	Tracking and letters to life insurance companies	3				120	
20	16 June 2012	Post letters to insurance companies, postage 3x recorded dely						£4.65
21	16 June 2012	Change estate net value sheet to add other cash items					30	
22	16 June 2012	Fill out IHT205(2006) and PA1 forms			2		90	
23	16 June 2012	Draft bank executor account forms					15	
24	20 June 2012	Cheque for probate office						£102.00
25								

Stats to date

Letters written: 10

Emails sent: 0

Forms filled in: 2

Phone calls made: 1

Hours on the job: 12

Money spent: £132

So far, so good. More next week...

Week 2

As the branches are local, I decided to personal visits to the bank and building society to hand over the letters informing them of the death, rather than use the post. There was, unexpectedly, quite a contrast in responses.

The bank adviser showed me into a side office as soon as I mentioned why I was there, and she was very well-prepared for such an occasion. She took the account details, made a call to their head office and gave me a reference number to quote to their 'estate department' should I have any queries during the process. She also offered the facility to have the funeral account paid for out of mother-in-law's funds (which were frozen from the date of her death), and explained in detail what I needed to do. My sister-in-law had paid a deposit to the funeral director from her own pocket, and it appeared to be a simple matter for the bank to reimburse her as well as settling the final account for the funeral when it became due. The adviser asked if I needed to open an Executor Account so we could keep all of the transactions made during probate separate to any other accounts. She gave me a booklet and the forms needed to open one should we decide to do that. Nothing seemed to be too much trouble, and I was most impressed.

The building society, though, was quite the opposite. No quiet side office, just a seat at a desk next to the main window looking out to people bustling about their business in the street beyond, and very little information offered. They took my letter, copied the death certificate and said they'd send it to their head office and I'd hear from them in two to three days. I asked for a reference number, or at least a standard receipt, to record the date I'd handed over the letter, but just received a blank stare. So I asked for the name of the adviser so I could say who I had given the letter to, should it be necessary, but it was a good few minutes before I could squeeze out his surname and jot it down. Quite a large proportion of mother-in-law's cash was lodged with the building society, and I began to wonder if this was going to turn out well.

Of the three insurance companies I wrote to last week, two were large well-known names. The third was a small institution, the policy having been taken out in 1921 when mother-in-law was one year old, for a halfpenny a week. Needless to say, that policy had become a paid-up decades ago. Guess which one sent a claim form and an information pack this week, before the large companies? The small one, of course.

I filled out the forms for the Executor Account, my sister-in-law and I signed them when they came over for a meal on Wednesday, and I took the forms back to the bank at the end of the week. A cheque had already arrived with a refund from the nursing home, for quite a substantial amount. So, we shall need the Executor Account sooner rather than later.

*Update. One other spreadsheet I found to be extremely useful was a 'Correspondence Tracker'. The purpose of this was to note all the letters/emails/phone calls made to and from each institution, so that I had a clear record of them. It also provided a simple means of noting down a temporary reminder of what should happen next, keep track of where more work was needed, and record when everything was complete for a particular institution. For instance, this was the final record for the Probate Office.

Probate Office	
20 June 2012	Probate and IHT forms sent
06 July 2012	Probate fee cheque cashed
11 July 2012	Email exchange regarding Executor 2 reserving power to apply for probate
13 July 2012	Probate information pack received
23 July 2012	Handed over probate forms and written Oath at probate hearing
06 August 2012	Grants of probate received
06 August 2012	COMPLETE

And this was the record for one of the insurance companies.

Wesleyan Insurance	
15 June 2012	Letter sent informing of death
19 June 2012	Acknowledgement letter received returning death certificate
23 June 2012	Claims pack received for two policies (probate required)
07 August 2012	Sent letter with claim forms and supporting documents
09 August 2012	Acknowledgement letter received returning death certificate and grant of probate
15 August 2012	Letter received with cheques
15 August 2012	COMPLETE

I believe this was a very worthwhile sheet to keep up to date, as it shows very clearly the current situation with each institution.

Not much time spent this week.

Stats to date

Letters written: 12

Emails sent: 1

Forms filled in: 3

Phone calls made: 1

Hours on the job: 15

Money spent: £138

Week 3

The bank was quick to open the Executor Account I'm pleased to say, and even though probate has yet to be completed there are three cheques in there already. Although the account has a 'both to sign' authority, it shows up on my internet banking page (with the same bank, of course). That's great, because I can check the transactions easily without having to trudge into town.

There was a snag here, which is worth knowing about if there are two executors. Contrary to instructions on the application form, the account was opened with my sister-in-law as the first party. This meant that all correspondence would go to her, some thirty miles away. I only spotted the error when I was casually looking over the introductory letter over a coffee in the town, and hot-footed it back to the bank. I don't think this was the first time this had happened, because they quickly came up with a solution which was to switch our addresses. At least that meant everything would come to me, although with my sister-in-law's name! I couldn't get too excited about the mistake as hopefully the account will only be open a few months, until the execution of the will is complete.

The first cheque was the refund from the nursing home. The fees were paid each month in advance, and there was a proportion of about 10/30ths due to the estate. They were extremely quick at sorting that out, as I'd had the cheque for some time. The other two cheques were from one of the three insurance companies, who paid out against the claim form without needing to see a grant of probate. The other large insurance company wrote this week to ask some very bizarre questions, almost as though they are looking for a way out. Why would they need the address of the person insured in 1949? OK, that was when one of the policies was taken out, but how many people would know where their mother-in-law lived over sixty years ago? Luckily we had her old National Identity Card, which had the information needed I thought that was a bit weird, and wondered what would have happened if we hadn't got that address.

The Department for Work and Pensions have written to say they owe the estate some money, and I've returned the form they sent me with the Executor Account details so they can transfer the funds direct. Similarly, one of the private pension companies have done the same and they have confirmed that the money they owe will be credited to the account at the end of the month.

Nothing at all has been received from the building society's head office after handing in the letter to the local branch advising of the death. So much for hearing in two to three days. I sent them an email this morning, so hopefully that will chivvy them up.

I have received confirmation of the date for the probate interview at the Bedford sub-registry, and the information pack arrived a couple of days ago. A copy of the oath is in the pack, with the details of the estate, the deceased and the will and there's a handy tick list to complete to confirm the details are correct.

It seems that at the interview the commissioner will simply check my identification, I will sign the original will and then swear the oath. The appointments are at five minute intervals, so I'm not expecting to be in there long.

Another snag here though. My sister-in-law (who is co-executor) is not available for the appointment so needs to sign a 'power reserved' form to indicate that she's happy for me to obtain probate, although wishes to reserve the right to complete the process later should I become indisposed. The form arrived only today with the pack, so I dropped it in the post first class hoping she would receive it and return it to me before she goes on holiday in two days time. Luckily by reading through the probate leaflets I saw this potential problem coming, and the probate office suggested I had her sign a letter with the same wording as the proper form and I already have that in my possession. The letter, if you want to have one up your sleeve, looks like this:

Address 1
Address 2
Post Code

12th July, 2012

Dear Sir or Madam,

Probate Application - (Dec'd)

This letter confirms that I am not applying for probate at the present time, but wish to have power reserved in case I need to apply in the future.

Yours faithfully,

Executor 2

Simple and to the point.

Overall then, everything is progressing quite well. The building society is lagging behind a bit, and hopefully the one remaining life insurance company will be content with my latest reply giving the 1949 address.

Stats to date

Letters written: 12

Emails sent: 1

Forms filled in: 7

Phone calls made: 4

Hours on the job: 20

Money spent: £146

Week 5

The appointment with the probate commissioner was set for 1240 on Monday. Slap bang in the middle of Bedford's lunchtime rush. We (my wife came as well as the probate instructions said family and friends were welcome) arrived at 1235, the security guard at the entrance to Bedford County Court asked 'Court or Probate?', and pointed to the appropriate waiting room.

No sooner had we sat down, when a chap called my name and we followed him into a cosy office with comfy chairs and a coffee table. No coffee, unfortunately. He asked for the copy of the oath (which contained details of the deceased and the estate value) and the checklist which I had already signed as requested before attending, then checked my identification. He knew to expect the PA25 form that my sister-in-law had signed to say she didn't want to be granted probate at the present time, so I handed that over. The letter I had prepared wasn't needed, because the postal system had performed well and the signed PA25 form made its return trip quicker than expected.

The commissioner then asked me to sign the reverse of mother-in-law's will and also the bottom of the oath. Finally, he asked would I like to swear or affirm the oath, handed me a bible and held a card which I had to read aloud (I swear by Almighty God…).

We were out at exactly 1240, five minutes after we'd entered the court building and at the time the appointment was supposed to start. Everything went very smoothly, and there was absolutely nothing to be concerned about. By far, the worst part was finding a parking space in the middle of Bedford at lunchtime.

So, the next significant event would be the receipt of twelve sealed copies of the grant of probate in a couple of weeks' time.

*Update. Note that they are not actually *sealed*; they are referred to as such because each one has the seal of the High Court impressed upon it.

Some progress was made this week by the remaining life assurance company. They sent a cheque in payment of a claim for one of the policies, so I must have quoted the correct address for mother-in-law's whereabouts in 1949. Nothing on the second policy though, which is rather worrying because in their latest letter they said it had been taken out by father-in-law and is therefore due to his estate (he passed away in 1993). I posted them a copy of the policy and a letter from the company received in 1992, both clearly stating that the life assured is mother-in-law. Let's see what they make of that!

Spent an entire morning mid-week looking for somewhere to make a colour double-sided A3 copy of the life policies taken out in 1921 (a penny a week) and 1926 (a halfpenny a week) with the Salvation Army Assurance Society Limited (now the Wesleyan). The policies are beautifully illuminated, and typical of legal documents from the early 20th century. Although they are by far the smallest value policies I am dealing with, the Wesleyan were alone in requiring me to send them the original copies to support the claim.

I managed to get good reproductions from a print shop in Stevenage Old Town. Actually, I walked passed them twice as the shop looked far to posh to be bothered with a couple of Xerox copies, but they were very helpful indeed and were happy to do the job at what I considered a reasonable price of around £7.

Stats to date

Letters written: 14

Emails sent: 4

Forms filled in: 8

Phone calls made: 6

Hours on the job: 23

Money spent: £150

Week 6

A major step forward this week, with payment of the second claim from the bigger of the three insurance companies. I had misunderstood the significance of a difference between proposer and life assured, it seems. The policy in question was taken out by father-in-law on the life of mother-in-law. Although he passed away about twenty years ago, it appears that on mother-in-law's death the insurance claim has to be made on behalf of *his* estate since he was the proposer.

It seems odd that a policy pays out to someone who has already died. I was also an executor for his will, so I could legitimately receive the payment and then distribute it according to his bequest. The cheque arrived early this week, so I plan to pay it into my bank account and then write cheques for the two legatees, making certain I have a good record of the three transactions to avoid any problems later. I will send out the cheques with an accompanying letter of explanation and a receipt to sign and return. The money has to be dealt with separately from mother-in-law's estate as it would at no time have been owned by her.

The final payment from one of mother-in-law's private pensions was paid into the Executor's Account as promised at the end of the month, so all pension payments owing have now been paid. Still nothing from the Attendance Allowance people about the three days overpayment. Mind you, the final pension was paid up until the date of the 'BD8' form issued by the registrar to send off to the Pensions Service, and I'm sure these agencies work in concert. So, if nothing is heard by the time the estate is ready for distribution, I think it would be safe to assume all is well.

On a happy note to end the week, I received a letter from the bank which was addressed to me, rather than my sister-in-law. So they have clearly corrected their records as promised.

Stats to date

Letters written: 17

Emails sent: 6

Forms filled in: 10

Phone calls made: 7

Hours on the job: 28

Money spent: £165

Right. Sealed grants of probate; where are you?

Week 7

The grant of probate arrived from Leicester Monday afternoon, together with the sealed copies. Our regular postman is on holiday and the post has been dropping on the mat about teatime, which has been a bit frustrating.

I spent that evening filling out the forms for the final insurance company claim, and the account closure request for mother-in-law's bank account and fixed rate bond, as well as preparing a data pack for the building society.

Come Tuesday morning, the insurance claim went off recorded delivery, as did the bank account and bond closure request. However, I made a personal visit to the building society as their advice had been a little sketchy. All seemed to go smoothly though. They took a copy of the sealed grant, scribbled a few notes and told me they'd have to send the copy to Head Office for approval. I asked them not to post me a cheque, as I wanted to pick it up personally so I could pay it into the Executor Account the same day. My phone number duly noted (not for the first time), I was promised a call as soon as approval came through.

I checked the Executor's Account on line Thursday morning, and the transfer of funds from the closed current account and fixed rate bond from the bank had been completed. That was quick! But no call from the building society.

I made a visit to the building society on Friday morning to see how things were going. Apparently they thought they'd called me to say everything was in order. I wasn't too bothered (although this wasn't the first time they'd messed up on the communications front), as the cashier appeared with a cheque blank and the copy of the grant they'd taken Tuesday. Half an hour later, I was presented with a cheque for the account balance. Any interest received after the date of death is liable for income tax, even if the account holder wasn't liable before. This was important, because I needed to know how much had been deducted so I could note that on the estate accounts.

I was getting wearisome of the tales about hearing from Head Office, but it wasn't a surprise to learn that the tax information would be in the closing statement at the end of the month. From Head Office. Now, I'm not usually one for putting on the charm, but I managed to persuade the cashier to check on her screen and make a note of the figures for me. She even agreed to make a copy of the cheque for my records so I could go straight to the bank without having to walk home first.

I took the cheque immediately to the bank and paid it into the Executor Account, thinking with it being a 'Building Society' cheque, it would clear quickly. However, I was told it would still take five working days. No great rush though as currently everything is ahead of schedule.

Suddenly, all the pieces seem to be coming together. Just a few more items to deal with. There's the statement of tax paid from the bank, which hopefully will arrive early next week. Then there's the claim to be paid by the third and final insurance company. Finally, there'll be the estate accounts to finish off and a careful check made on any tax liability for the Inland Revenue. Following that will come distribution of the legacies.

Stats to date

Letters written: 19

Emails sent: 6

Forms filled in: 13

Phone calls made: 7

Hours on the job: 31

Money spent: £168

Looking forward to next week!

Week 8

The final life insurance claim has been paid, and the company responded favourably to my request to return the magnificent policy documents. So, I have the originals for the family history file and didn't need to have them copied after all. Still, I had no idea at the time whether or not the company may have insisted upon consigning them to the shredder.

So, all the cheques and transfers have now been paid into the Executor Account, and the account has a fully cleared balance. I asked the bank to send me a closing statement of mother-in-law's current account and fixed rate bond so I could note the tax deducted from interest paid on the bond since the date of death.

A statement turned up on Friday, but it just showed the interest paid, nothing about tax. The monthly interest amounts look about the same as they had been while mother-in-law was alive, so I suspected they hadn't deducted any tax. A quick phone call to the bank's estates team confirmed that tax would most certainly have been taken off. I asked if they could give me the figures over the phone, but apparently I will have to wait for a printed statement of tax paid. About a week, they said.

Actually, I still reckoned they have just paid the interest free of tax, which will be a nuisance because it means I will have to contact the Inland Revenue and pay any tax due before I can complete the accounts and distribute the legacies. That could take an age!

Hopefully I am wrong about the tax, which would mean the amount owing to the tax man from the estate during the administration period is already settled, and I can simply complete the estate accounts and have the legatees sign them off. If not, though, I'm expecting a few more weeks of protracted communications before everything is settled.

Ah, forgot to say about the funeral director hiccup! Remember when I reported mother-in-law's death to her bank, they offered to settle the funeral account out of her frozen funds? When the time came, I forwarded the funeral account to the estates team at the bank. My sister-in-law had paid a substantial deposit, so I asked them to reimburse her and then settle the balance with the funeral director. I know she received her cheque about three weeks ago, so was surprised to get a reminder from the funeral director on Monday. I called them immediately and they confirmed that no payment had been received. The bank's estates team were very helpful though when I rang them again. They called the funeral director themselves, stopped the original cheque and sent out a new one. There was something quite discomforting about being chased for the payment of a funeral account, but on Friday I received a receipt to say the account had been paid. So that is now definitely settled.

Stats to date
Letters written: 20
Emails sent: 6
Forms filled in: 13
Phone calls made: 10
Hours on the job: 33
Money spent: £174

Here's hoping that the tax situation won't cause a hiatus on what has been quite a smooth path so far!

Week 9

What a frustrating week! Haven't moved forward one little bit. Still awaiting the statement of tax paid on mother-in-law's bank accounts since the date of death, so I can work out whether or not there is anything more due to the Inland Revenue from the estate. Phoned the bank twice, and on Friday was delighted to hear that it had been sent. Until, that is, I heard the end of the sentence. Today. Friday. So, not only did it not turn up early to midweek as promised last time I phoned, it wasn't even sent until the end of the week! Tried again to get them to give me the figures over the phone, but they refused.

As I had always suspected, the time that probate takes is little to do with the amount of work involved (remember I have only spent about 33 man-hours so far), and everything to do with waiting for organisations to respond.

I have no idea at present whether the estate accounts can be completed without further ado, or whether I am going to need to fill out a tax form (R27) and wait for the tax man to work out the amount payable.

All this cash sitting in the Executor Account meant that there was no interest being earned on the estate balance, so it seemed prudent to make a partial distribution to allow the legatees to make the best of the funds available. So, I distributed the bulk of the estate to the beneficiaries, just holding back enough to pay the expenses incurred carrying out probate, and to settle any tax which may be due. And a bit spare, just in case.

Almost all the estate value took the form of cash, apart from a couple of furniture items and jewellery. The furniture was of little value and we donated it to the care home where mother-in-law had spent her final days. She would have been happy that we had done that. The distribution of her jewellery was also straightforward, because there was a list, carefully written, left with the will. This not only stated which items should go to whom, but also why she had decided who should be given each piece and why it was important to her. Needless to say, the distribution was emotionally charged.

Stats to date

Letters written: 20

Emails sent: 6

Forms filled in: 13

Phone calls made: 11

Hours on the job: 35

Money spent: £174

Week 10

Nothing happened.

Not a single thing.

Stats to date

Letters written: 20

Emails sent: 6

Forms filled in: 13

Phone calls made: 11

Hours on the job: 35

Money spent: £174

Week 11

The tax certificate arrived from the bank, but it was for tax paid on interest from the beginning of this tax year to the date of death in June. That was wrong on two counts. First, the interest was being paid gross up until the date of death (I know, because the amount received each month was correct) and second, what I had requested was a certificate showing the tax paid on the interest between the date of death and the closure of account on August 9th. Even though an R85 form had been lodged to receive gross interest on the account, anything received after the date of death became the property of the estate and so attracted tax at the standard rate. I needed to know how much had been paid in order to complete the estate accounts and settle any unpaid tax. Later in the week, the correct certificate arrived. It showed that tax had been paid on the interest, so there's no messing about to do with the Inland Revenue. Hurrah!

Now that the estate accounts are complete, I can make the final distributions, and pay myself the expenses I've incurred over the last few weeks. These are for telephone calls, postage and the probate fees. My time was for free, naturally.

I prepared a summary of the estate accounts for the two legatees, and asked them to check the figures and to sign a declaration that they agree with them, and that I will not be held liable for any errors found in the future. This is the summary (with the actual figures replaced by notional amounts).

Estate Account Summary for the Late

CAPITAL ACCOUNT			
Receipts ***(assets at date of death)***			
Bank 1	£1,234.56		
Bank 2	£1,234.56		
Building Society 1	£1,234.56		
		£3,703.68	
Insurance Company 1	£1,234.56		
Insurance Company 2	£1,234.56		
Insurancy Company 3	£251.72		
		£2,720.84	
Balance of state pension	£123.45		
Balance of Private Pension	£123.45		
Nursing Home refund of payment	£1,234.56		
		£1,481.46	
Surplus from Income Account		£444.42	
		£8,350.40	
Liabilities			
Funeral account deposit paid		£1,000.00	
Funeral account		£1,717.75	
POA expenses to date of death - Attorney 1	£9.65		
POA expenses to date of death - Attorney 2	£80.73		
Executor's expenses (inc Probate £102) - 1	£176.48		
Executor's expenses - 2	£20.00		
		£286.86	
		£3,004.61	
Balance (Receipts-Liabilities) to Distribution Account			£5,345.79

INCOME ACCOUNT				
Receipts ***(since date of death)***				
	gross	tax paid	received	
Current a/c interest since DoD	£0.00	£0.00	£0.00	
1-Year Bond a/c interest since DoD	£123.45	£24.69	£98.76	
Building Society a/c interest since DoD	£123.45	£24.69	£98.76	
		£49.38	£197.52	£197.52
Attendance Allowance paid 13th June, 2012				£123.45
Premium Bonds cashed, paid 13th June, 2012				£123.45
				£444.42
Payments ***(since date of death)***				
Executor's Account charges			£0.00	
Income tax payable			£0.00	
				£0.00
Surplus to Capital Account				£444.42

DISTRIBUTION ACCOUNT			
Balance from Capital Account			£5,345.790
Half share to Legatee 1	£2,672.895		
Half share to Legatee 2	£2,672.895		
			£5,345.790

RELEASE, RECEIPT, AND INDEMNITY

The signatories hereby acknowledge receipt of one half interest in the residuary estate of and hereby release and forever discharges in his capacity as executor of the estate of , and of any and all claims of any kind which the distributee ever had, now has or hereafter can, shall or may have, under the Last Will and Testament of the decedent and with respect to the administration of the estate of decedent.

The distributees acknowledge that they have been provided with sufficient disclosure with respect to the terms, provisions, costs of administration and asset allocation prepared by executor. The signatories hereby indemnify the executor from any and all liability resulting from the accounting and asset allocation in connection with the estate

Estate accounts approved:

Legatee 1

Legatee 2

Final stats

Letters written: 22

Emails sent: 6

Forms filled in: 13

Phone calls made: 11

Hours on the job: 37

Money spent: £175

And that's it.

Probate complete.

Final Thoughts

The process took eleven weeks, which is better than the three month target I set myself. This compares very favourably with my first hand experience of using professionals to carry out probate, which has ranged from nine months to over a year. Time actually spent doing things came to about 37 hours, although I'm sure I missed logging a few hours just checking over records, updating spreadsheets, re-writing letters, and picking up and putting down activities. Call it 40 hours. That's about a week's work in terms of a proper job.

Expenses ended up at £175, which included £102 for probate fees, £7 for professional A3 copying, £7 for certified extra copies of the death certificate and £7 for a book on how to do probate! The rest was for telephone calls and postage (everything went 'Signed For', so this added up to quite a tidy sum).

In total, I filled in 13 forms, ranging from claiming state pension and private pension owed, through the probate and inland revenue forms, to opening the Executor Account at the bank. None of these were difficult to understand.

The 22 letters written included the initial ones sent to inform the various institutions of mother-in-law's death, responding to enquiries from the insurance companies, and liaising with the estates department at the bank. In addition, there were six emails and eleven phone calls, although I tried to stick to letters where I could to make sure I had a record of the whole process.

Would I do it again? Oh, yes. It's given me an interesting insight into how probate works from start to finish. I think even if there had been a house to sell (the house had already sold under power of attorney prior to the death) or stocks and shares to be valued and disposed of, the process would have been quite straightforward. It would have taken longer, of course, particularly as initiating the sale of a house for example would have to await grant of probate.

I hope that by reading this, you will have gained enough confidence to have a go at carrying out probate yourself. If you can follow instructions, write letters, do basic sums, are well organised and can keep accurate records, there's really no need to spend thousands of pounds on professional assistance.

Summing Up - List of Main Activities

Find the will, insurance policies, investments, etc.

Jot down a list of assets and debts

Read as many 'How To' guides as possible

Create a provisional estate value

Inform institutions of death (banks, pension providers, insurance companies, etc.)

Download support leaflets and forms from probate office and inland revenue

Fill out and send probate and inheritance tax forms

Arrange probate registry appointment

Open Executor Account with bank

Attend probate registry to swear the oath

When grant of probate arrives, send sealed copies to bank, insurance companies, etc. with claim forms

Receive payments of money owed to the estate

Check tax status of any income since death

Compile final estate account

Pay outstanding debts and expenses

Distribute legacies according to the will

By the same author:

Whomerley Wood Moat, Stevenage

- The House in the Clearing

WHOMERLEY WOOD MOAT
STEVENAGE

THE HOUSE
IN THE CLEARING

Philip Wadner

Believed to have been the home of the de Homeley family in the late thirteenth century, the site of the medieval moated homestead in Whomerley Wood, Stevenage is located about one and a half miles almost due south of the original Saxon settlement around where St. Nicholas Church stands today. Evidence of medieval life has been found there, and excavations on the island have also uncovered relics from Roman times. The author has sifted through a huge variety of sources, and has knitted together facts, suppositions and his personal reflections to create a powerful image of times gone by.

Find out more and buy at www.cadebooks.co.uk

www.ingramcontent.com/pod-product-compliance
Ingram Content Group UK Ltd.
Pitfield, Milton Keynes, MK11 3LW, UK
UKHW020233250726
13967UKWH00001B/350

9 780993 198717